CHEMICALS
between us

USA TODAY BESTSELLING AUTHOR
PERSEPHONE AUTUMN

BETWEEN WORDS PUBLISHING LLC

CHEMICALS
between us

USA TODAY BESTSELLING AUTHOR
PERSEPHONE AUTUMN

BETWEEN WORDS PUBLISHING LLC

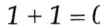

$$1 + 1 = 0$$

BOOKS BY persephone autumn

LAKE LAVENDER SERIES

Depths Awakened

One Night Forsaken

Every Thought Taken

DEVOTION SERIES

Distorted Devotion

Undying Devotion

Beloved Devotion

Darkest Devotion

Sweetest Devotion

BAY AREA DUET SERIES

<u>Click Duet</u>

Through the Lens

Time Exposure

<u>Inked Duet</u>

Fine Line

Love Buzz

<u>Insomniac Duet</u>

Restless Night

A Love So Bright

<u>Artist Duet</u>

Blank Canvas

Abstract Passion

<u>Novellas</u>

Reese

Penny

STONE BAY SERIES

Broken Sky—Prequel

Shattered Sun

Fractured Night

Fallen Stars

Stolen Dreams

Raptured Souls

Tethered Hearts

Fiery Storm

STANDALONE ROMANCE NOVELS

Sweet Tooth

Transcendental

In Knots For You

POETRY COLLECTIONS

Ink Veins

Broken Metronome

Slipping From Existence

Poisonous Heart

Beneath Wildflowers

Chemicals Between Us

PUBLISHED UNDER P. AUTUMN

STANDALONE NON-ROMANCE NOVELS

By Dawn

CONTENTS

CONTENT & *author's note*

Chemicals Between Us is a contemporary poetry collection. Please be aware it contains sensitive subjects that may trigger emotional distress in some readers. If you are sensitive to the listed triggers, this story may not be for you.

Please use your own personal judgement before proceeding.

- Mental health - depression and anxiety
- Heartbreak
- Grief
- Other possible dark elements

If you or someone you know struggles with depression and/or anxiety, or has experienced grief (relationship or physical loss), I encourage you to connect with a professional who is trained to help.

Resources are available online at psychologytoday.com/us/therapists **or** nimh.nih.gov/health/find-help. If you're in need of immediate help, call or text 988 or visit https://988life line.org/

Take care of yourself and those you hold close.

I love you,

Persephone

I just knew

I remember that day
so many years ago.
I entered the unfamiliar room,
and you were already there
poised
radiant
a force I somehow knew.
I didn't question it,
I had zero doubts,
but by some unknown flicker of intuition
I just knew
you'd be more.
And on that day,
so many years ago,
I was right.

battle of wills

It's interesting,
the small but big moments you remember.
Those first glances,
the first time your hand grazed mine,
the teasing
and laughter
and not-so-subtle way you let me know
you wanted me.
But I didn't make it easy,
almost refused to, actually.
Not because
I didn't reciprocate
or want you just as desperately
or crave your touch
your taste
the feel of your skin pressed to mine.
No, I fought those urges
that hunger
that fevered desperation
because I'd been broken before,
shredded by someone who claimed to love me.
So I put up my shields,
stacked brick after brick around my heart
until the walls were impossibly high.

Little did I know,
you came prepared.
With a fierce determination,
you scaled those walls,
went over the edge
and battled for my heart.
Eventually, my resistance
was for show
evaporated
morphed into acceptance.
You fought for me,
and when I look back on it now,
that steely resolution
that intense, purposeful strength
is what shattered my defenses.

acceptance

Before you,
I don't remember a time
when many people in my life
accepted me exactly
as I am
for what I love
for what I have to offer.
And then you walked into my world.
Bold.
Ambitious.
A glorious, beautiful sunrise
to complement my dark nights.
But more than anything,
you welcomed
every side of me
my baggage
what I brought to the table.
With arms wide open, you
accepted me
encouraged me
gave me the opportunity to
bloom
flourish
explore.

I'll never forget…
the easy way you
believed in me,
the effortless way you
embraced my weird,
the straightforward way you
supported my dreams,
the simple way you
accepted *me*.

paradox

The irony of
being with someone who made me question every
thought,
decision,
action,
move I made,
to being with someone who helped me believe in every
thought,
decision,
action,
move I made.
For years,
and to this day,
I still struggle with
the utter paradox
the complete opposition
the absolute contradiction of it all.
Because… how?
From avoided to pursued,
ignored to worshipped,
mocked to respected,
tolerated to coveted.
How could I not question
everything?

But you held strong,
pushed through my barriers,
pieced together my infinite puzzle,
showed me what *real* connection was.
And when I questioned the
contradiction
inconsistency
discrepancy of it all,
you let me spill my thoughts without interruption,
and then you
soothed
reassured
vowed
that was all in my past
that would not be the future.
It took years to believe it,
to be convinced,
to accept it as truth.
And then...
the future became the past.
Again.

more than friends

For weeks,
we toed the line
flirted with the possibility
danced around the obvious.
You knew,
as did I,
we were on the way to
more,
but neither of us admitted
that very real truth
aloud.
But the inevitability of what would happen
existed,
and once we stopped fighting fate,
it took on a life of its own.
Late at night,
in early Spring,
you backed me against my car,
closed the distance between us,
and changed
everything.
In that singular moment,
all I felt was
your soft lips

the sweep of your tongue
your gentle yet firm grip
your hunger.
All I knew was
you couldn't get enough,
and neither could I.
One kiss and I
ignited
sparked to life
melted in your arms
found a light in the dark
silently begged it never end.
Years later,
that life-altering night feels like a
fever dream.
A vivid picture I play
over and over
in my mind.
A memory I will
pin in my mental scrapbook,
tuck away for safekeeping.
Only now,
the light has dimmed,
the hunger has faded,
and we are back to
"friends."

always yes

People-pleasing,
it runs in my veins,
and yours.
The consistent urge to
make others happy,
never step on toes,
never let anyone down,
always give a piece of yourself away,
always say yes.
But saying yes to you, it was
different
effortless
as easy as breathing.
So when you asked that life-altering question,
I didn't question how easily
I said yes.
Never had that three-letter word felt so
simple
right
fulfilling
perfect.
Without an ounce of doubt in my soul,
I said yes
and thought I'd never say anything else.

Because with you,
yes wasn't said to
please
comfort
appease.
With you,
yes was
true
resolute
unerring.
Always.

evolution

The progression of
us
was anything but
a slow evolution.
But only because,
before you,
nothing felt so
certain
real
absolute.
For the first time,
I didn't question the future
I didn't fear what would happen next
I wasn't afraid to be myself
I wasn't scared to love or be loved.
So
I leaped headfirst
into you
into us
into the unknown
without an ounce of trepidation.
I basked in
our evolution
the rapid whirlwind

the new path we chose to hike.
I cherished your acceptance
of me
of my life
of my history,
and did my damnedest to reciprocate
your incredible gift.
Some say our evolution was
hasty
unexpected
impetuous.
And maybe it was.
But our evolution was also
fire
passion
strength
courage
light
love
everything.

combustible

From the start,
we were a ticking time bomb of
intrigue
heat
lust
connection
inevitability.
Every moment together was
fascinating
undiluted
scorching
addictive
real.
And for the longest time,
I didn't think it was possible to
feel anything as powerful
extinguish the persistent flame
lose the intensity.
But like all things combustible,
our fire started to
flicker
fade
snuff out.
Our once unstoppable fire became

a neglected ember,
fighting for oxygen
begging for kindling
weeping to not become ash.
The beginning was
incendiary
bright
fierce,
but it didn't take long for our flame to
dim
dissolve
disappear completely.
Once combustible,
now flame resistant.

the first shadow

At the time, I was
too distracted
too intrigued
too blinded by rose-colored glasses
to see
the first shadow.
It was subtle,
an almost indiscernible vignette
ghosting the edges
of us,
but it was there, nonetheless.
As time ticked by,
as I reflected on that moment,
I saw that
illusive first shadow
dancing in the periphery.
Yet, I didn't acknowledge it,
not fully,
fearing the truth of what it meant.
Instead, I chose to
be willfully blind
see the positive
not make something from what might have been
    nothing.

But
the shadow still existed,
and over time,
the first shadow
darkened
expanded
morphed
until one shadow
became two
and two became three…
And still,
I adopted ignorance
I elected not to see
I opted for fantasy over reality.

the start of forever

Swirls of color,
hints of glitter,
subtle rock music,
this was the start of forever.
Quiet,
intimate,
simple,
meaningful.
I still carry a picture from
the start of forever
in my wallet,
tucked safely behind cards
to preserve that day.
A day that now
stings the backs of my eyes
squeezes the straining organ in my chest
tears off a piece of my soul.
It was a beautiful night,
the start of forever.
But now, it is
a handful of photos
a few paragraphs of words
a story no longer shared
as the start of forever.

pride

Loud and unabashedly,
I was proud
to be yours
to be your sidekick
to hold your hand
to tell people you were my wife.
My heart swelled
at your brilliance
at your thoughtful nature
at your level of devotion
at the idea of being yours forever.
When it came to you,
your strength
your tenacity
your unique idiosyncrasies
your logical mind
and sarcastic tongue,
I was
awestruck
bewitched
intimidated
seduced
aroused.
But most of all,

I was
honored.
During the most significant years of my life,
you were mine
and nothing else mattered.

dreams

There is no singular definition for
dreams,
yet, I feel as though
sometimes I experience them
all at once.
Ideal
perfect
the imagination of events, people, places
hopes, wishes
an idle fantasy, a daydream
a nightmare
a vision of the future
the possibility of more.
And sometimes,
I feel as though
I no longer experience
any of them.
That my time for dreams
is over, gone
has passed its preprinted expiration date.
But every now and again,
there is a glimmer of
hope
the ideal

perfection
a future.
Not of the one stitched in my mind years ago,
but of something
new
simple
untainted
attainable
resuscitative.
Dreams are an unstable tightrope,
a tricky, unsteady notion of
anticipation
expectation
ambition
standards so high you can't breathe.
But dreams are also
opportunity
possibility
desire
confidence
inspiration
the most profound, fundamental breath you'll ever take.

silence

There is something so
restorative
peaceful
provocative
confrontational
restless
unpleasant
formidable
about sitting alone in silence.
Too many times, I begged for
silence to reflect
a single moment to process
a breath or heartbeat to digest,
and somehow my appeal was interpreted as
a plea for solitude
a request to withdraw
a need for separation.
And so I was
isolated
stranded
abandoned
in the chaotic, swirling centrifuge of my warped,
   catastrophic thoughts.
Before long, the silence was

familiar
typical
predicted
promised,
and I no longer wanted it.
But it was too late.
The definition of silence had been
changed
reshaped
misconstrued
dissected
slashed
until it was unrecognizable.
Slowly, incontestably, silence became
the shadows I couldn't escape
the path to heartbreak
a punishment for something out of my control.
And in the end, silence became
a weapon
a form of retribution
commonplace
paralyzing.

price tag

In a random twist of fate,
every love I've had
has always come with
a price tag.
Square and plain and small,
dark ink on bleached paper,
on sale on bold, bright stickers.
The perfect gift to
atone for missed time
offset guilt
distract
attempt to mend the continuously expanding divide.
From a young age,
I knew the
power of
weight of
definition of
a price tag.
And it seems,
even now,
there is no love
that doesn't come with one.
Not even,
the forever kind.

locked down, locked out

As for so many,
everything changed during
lockdown.
In those first few months of
chaos
confusion
unpredictability,
we continued to thrive.
A new path was presented,
and we navigated it with
confidence
persistence
some frazzled nerves
together
…until pandemonium ensued.
One event,
one swift change in the code,
one day of utter, complete mayhem,
was the first step toward the fault line.
With a sympathetic, attentive heart, I offered
breathing room
an ear
a shoulder
to take on more.

Although it brought relief,
with it came newfound
consequences.
The demons of the past
emerged
commandeered
haunted
seized.
I understood the why,
but the answer didn't make it
hurt any less
easier to handle
not as scary.
And soon, with slow, delicate precision, the demons
used their voice
made their mark
splintered my heart
sketched irreversible memories
locked me out.
Still, I continued to
fight for you
stay with you
love you.
Because you were always
worth the battle
worth the wait
worth the risk
worthy of my heart.

shitstorm

I woke up today and all I heard was
noise
sounds of annoyance
scrapes and scratches
a slight tick in the air.
Tick
Tick
Tick
It swam around me,
a clusterfuck
a shitstorm,
swirling like a tornado
in my head
everywhere I went.
I woke up today and
wished I never did
wished the darkness would just
swallow me whole
take me away from
all the noise
all the false promises
all the fading dreams.
Tomorrow.
Just let me sleep.

optimism in the dark

As a lifelong pessimist,
it's uncanny to find
optimism in the dark.
Yet, I did.
High and low I
searched
hunted
rummaged
for an ounce of light.
And when I found it, I
reveled
praised
mentally cried happy tears.
Because that light felt like
hope
restoration
evolution.
So I clutched that light with mighty fists,
kept it close to my chest,
nurtured it often and fully.
I gave
and gave
and gave.
For a time, that precious dose of optimism was

sustainable
enough
priceless
immaculate.
And during that time, I allowed myself to believe in
hope
revitalization
new beginnings.

the second shadow

Depression is a fickle bitch
who slowly gnaws at your soul
until it makes you believe
your darkest thoughts are
true.
Between shadows one and two,
the occasional cloud cover drifted by,
masking reality
hinting at the truth
tickling the edges of my mind.
Still,
I ignored it.
Preoccupied with stories and daydreams,
I was determined to
stay positive
only see the good
live life to the fullest
believe everything was okay.
In the end,
my optimistic heart paid the price
my tender soul suffered the consequences
my life went in the opposite direction.
The second shadow should have
woken me up

screamed louder in my head
waved bigger signs with bolder letters.
Maybe then, I would have
seen what was right in front of me
recognized the truth for what it was
tried a different tactic.
But I didn't.

false hope

In the periphery,
hope simmered
and sparkled
and teased me with abandon.
Oh, how easily
I fell into its waiting arms
and embraced its warmth.
Because god,
did I want to believe something
better
incredible
life changing
was on the horizon.
Oh, how I needed that
glimmer of hope
light in the dark
inkling of reassurance
hint of anticipation.
It kept my heart beating,
it made my dreams soar,
it whispered quietly that all would be okay.
But like a venomous serpent
slithering through the brush,
hope had its proverbial fangs out,

poised,
ready to strike.
And like the wistful escapist I am,
I didn't feel it when
its fangs sunk deep
the venom started to spread.
Instead, I lived in a rainbow-colored bubble of
false hope.

shallow grave

White flags waving,
neon signs flashing,
voices in my head screaming
as I dropped to the floor and
stared at nothing for hours.
It was a sign,
a silent, desperate cry for help,
that I waved off with another
"I'm fine."
An answer you
accepted too easily
heard and walked off
didn't question.
I wish you would have pushed me to talk,
I wish you would have insisted I tell you
the dark and dangerous thoughts in my head,
I wish you would have wrapped me in your arms
and held me to your chest
and whispered soft promises
like you did once before.
Instead,
you walked away,
thinking I'd be better with my thoughts.
And as I lay on that gray-and-white rug,

eyes dry
stomach churning
soul withering,
I thought of countless ways to end up
in a shallow grave.

one—two punch

Unexpectedly,
devastation hit like a
one–two punch.
A fierce and shocking blow to the
solar plexus
heart
soul.
Though you were
shattered, you
shouldered the weight
became the caretaker
made lists and checked off items.
Your world had been
rattled
broken
turned on its head,
but you held strong.
I loved and
admired and
envied
your ability to persevere during difficult times.
I have never been,
nor will I ever be,
that resilient or steady.

Because on those days,
while you were away,
I felt
isolated
left out of the fold
forgotten.
I know it was
selfish
disgraceful
inconsiderate
fucked up,
but it doesn't change the truth.
While you consoled others,
all I wanted was to
wrap you in my arms
and love you.

Stitched and frayed

The first real sign of forever,
again,
started to stitch my weary soul
back together.
A dream,
a promise,
a way to leave all the darkness behind.
I won't deny the way it
taxed my every heartbeat
took a toll on my body
made me question my sanity daily.
But I shouldered each
ache
pain
mental burden
for the end result.
A chance to reset,
a chance at more and forever.
As one end of my threadbare soul
frayed,
the other end
slowly pieced itself back together,
hopeful and exhilarated.
In that pocket of time, I chose

happiness
anticipation
confidence
the unexpected.
I stepped into the unknown with my head high
and a naive mind
as I wished for what once was
once more.

organized chaos

I've always been the type to
rearrange my life
shift things around
try something new
for everyone but myself.
But on a day in late June,
as I stood in the thick of chaos,
I did one of the things
I do best.
Organized.
Type *A*, brain crazed and overwhelmed,
I pushed
every muscle to its limit
every bone until it ached
every cell until it cried *no more.*
I did it to
clean
find normal
occupy my restless mind.
But most of all,
I did it to
please you.
And for the tiniest fraction,
for the faintest blip,

I bore witness to your
delight
disbelief
awe,
and it made my heart soar.
With the physical cloud of chaos lifted,
I believed everything would
be okay
fall into place.
And for a heartbeat,
it did.

fear

A swirling fire in the solar plexus,
burning
churning
expanding
overwhelming
rooting deep.
Anxiety and I have always been familiar,
since I was young,
always anticipating the worst
at every turn.
But this all-consuming
fear
gnawed at my aura
nibbled at my soul
fed off my insides
with a wicked grin on its lips.
I fought against it,
shoved at it with all my might,
forced it into a small box in the back of my mind,
but it didn't matter.
Fear is a
cruel beast
motherfucker
searing brand

virus
systemic meltdown,
and I wasn't strong enough to
fight against it.
Still,
I tried and
I cried and
I lied.
Because this version of fear had
intricate layers
different faces
volatile bursts
occasional tenderness
claws in my heart.
I didn't want fear to
take over
consume me
win.
So I let the fear in,
I drowned in its toxic venom,
until I no longer wanted to breathe.

rainbow

The news broke with a
swift, sickening punch to the solar plexus.
With your feisty, rebellious spirit,
I thought we still had
years
a lifetime.
But like those before you,
a malignant monster
rooted so very deep
had other plans.
Three years and a day
after your brother,
a year and a half
after your sister,
you followed their footsteps and
crossed the big rainbow in the sky.
And fuck, it was
hard
devastating
a critical turning point.
For days and weeks, I swear
I heard you in the room
I saw you walk by
I felt you at my side.

But you weren't there,
no one was there,
and this is when
I started to lose
myself
my purpose
my reason.
Because after I said goodbye to you,
affection
attention
interaction of any kind
was rare,
and I suppose
we were grieving in our own ways,
just never together.
I miss your spitfire soul
and late-in-life tender heart
and wish you could've rolled in the evergreens longer.

lost

In unfamiliar territory,
we drifted in different directions
physically
mentally
wholly.
As the rift grew wider,
as we lost ourselves to our demons,
as I dropped lower down the list,
I lost myself.
The darkness didn't come all at once,
I know this now.
The darkness slithered in
over the years and
embedded itself in the cracks,
waiting
infesting
devouring
until there was nothing of me left
until I was no more.
Suffocated by loneliness,
drowned by guilt,
consumed by failure,
the darkness thrilled with delight.
Still,

I took another breath,
I swam for the surface,
I pushed myself harder,
because I didn't want to fail
because I didn't want to lose
because I didn't want to surrender.
I was lost and
I wanted you to find me
I wanted you to find us
again.
But as day after day passed
like red Xs on a paper calendar in the kitchen,
it felt like you didn't want to
find me
find us
again.

jealousy

Until you, I never experienced
true jealousy.
But magically, you
stoked the fire
added more kindling
brought out my inner green-eyed monster.
Ironically,
the foundation of my jealousy was built with
the same bricks that
held my heart captive.
For years,
you assured me
your heart was mine.
But those villainous demons
in my mind
made me question the validity of those words.
Maybe it was with a warped perspective that
I picked up on
things that weren't there.
Or maybe,
I witnessed
a glimpse of reality.
Because with a select few,
I swear you

smiled
flirted
cared more than a friend.
And I only wonder this because,
once upon a time,
you gifted me with those exact same
attributes.
Not once did you
pick up on
my discomfort
my oncoming distress
my jealousy.
And it makes me
question
if you were actually
smiling
flirting
caring for them more than a friend
with me at your side.

silence, again

It was most interesting how
the one time I needed your
strength
embrace
voice
resilience,
you only gave me
silence.
My life felt like
an endless battle
a continuous cry for help
another step closer to the cliffside,
and you were
silent.
I was not the only one
struggling,
but it felt like
I was the only one
trying
to keep *us* going.
And I was exhausted by
giving so much
trying so hard

caring
when you didn't seem to.
So while you stayed silent,
I plunged deeper
into the darkest abyss.

give me darkness

Soft sheets, warm blankets
I lay alone,
crying
begging for sleep,
the dreamless type
the one you never wake from.
Oh, how I ache
for love
for darkness
for quiet
for a peace that will settle my maddened soul.
Please take this bone-deep exhaustion,
please release the shackles on my tortured spirit,
please set me free,
please
please
please.
I am so tired
of being a burden, an inconvenience
of being an afterthought, no one's priority
of being lonely, unwanted
of never being enough for anyone, not even myself.
I'm tired

of being loved when it's convenient
of being…

lonely

Time and again,
over the years,
I expressed my
loneliness.
And in those earlier years,
you gifted me with
an apology
and promised time together.
I basked in those
precious minutes
when I had you to myself.
But with each passing day,
those moments became more
fleeting
rare
nonexistent.
And for the longest time, I
understood why
forgave you for your absence
didn't push or complain or nag
let the divide expand.
Because when I spoke up,
all it seemed to do was
frustrate

irritate
perpetuate
an already painful situation.
So, against every
instinct I had
cell in my body
fragment of my soul,
I closed my mouth and bit my tongue.
And at a certain point,
I convinced myself I was
destined
for loneliness.
Seems,
this time,
I was right.

almost end

To adjust to the new
us,
you packed a bag,
got in your car,
and drove away for two weeks.
I get the reason why.
You were in pain,
you wanted to sort through your feelings
away from me,
you needed to figure out how to
move on.
But with your absence, I
withered
cracked
shattered
lost all sense of reality.
While you were gone,
I prepared for the end.
I thought about the
how
when
where
more times than I'll admit aloud.
I organized and

stacked and
made things easier to manage
for my nonexistence.
But as I gave the idea full merit,
as I considered the possibility of
how
when
where,
three reasons stopped me from taking
the step.
Munchkin, Dad, and you.
You'd experienced so much in such a short period,
you were about to experience more
because of me,
and the thought of hurting you
in the worst possible way
kept me from
the almost end.
You.

chemicals between us

It's okay
to be sad
to ache
to cry and cry and cry.
It's okay to feel
hollow
hurt
splintered
like a fraction of a soul.
It's okay to be
angry
flustered
shaky
hot
irrational
over what is
was
could have been.
It isn't you,
and it isn't me.
Of all things, what
formed a wedge
slowly pulled us apart
shifted us from united to individualistic

divided us,
was the
chemicals between us.
The demons neither of us could
quiet
suppress
appease
satiate
vanquish
are the same monsters that
wouldn't let us rediscover our
light
harmony
peace
happily ever after.
The biggest irony of all...
chemistry brought us together
and chemistry is what ripped us apart.

"friends"

When I knew change was
necessary
crucial
vital,
I told you what I needed.
And it hurts that every idea you offered,
never included you.
They were
a well-used bandage
a single stitch for a gaping wound
a one-ply tissue for a puddle.
And sadly,
it confirmed
what I often refused to admit.
We had gone from
never getting enough of each other
to
a contractual obligation.
The moment I garnered
courage
to speak up,
you listened and seemed indifferent.
In that exact moment,
I knew it was the end.

Because I shared my pain,
and you shared solutions that didn't
include you.
Instead,
you asked to remain
friends.
Since that moment,
you've barely been
an acquaintance.
But what hurts most is
your carefree dismissal
how forgettable I am
the clinical way you regard me
that we are the furthest from friends.

grief

I always thought of grief as
the feelings you experience
after a physical death.
But now I know
differently
unequivocably
that grief has outstretched wings
that grief defies boundaries.
Grief is a
rusty, dull blade to the heart
that twists again and again
to remind you of what is
lost
gone
never coming back.
Since before our paths unraveled,
I grieved you.
Until I was brave enough to look back,
I missed what was right in front of me.
For so long, you were
absent
hurting
shutting me out
abandoning me.

Not to hurt me,
never to intentionally wound me,
but to save pieces of yourself.
Part of me knew this,
but I ignored the niggling voice
for love
and to help you.
To this day,
with every molecule in my body,
I love you.
But I also
mourn you
grieve you
forgive you
wish you nothing but happiness.

the loss of you

It's funny…
the things you miss
when you lose someone.
Simple reminders of
a life together
a life you no longer live.
It feels like one of those dreams
nightmares
where you wander
aimlessly
endlessly
looking for someone.
And just when you find them,
just when they're within reach,
the dream
shifts
fades
morphs
into something else.
Something unsettling and foreign.
And no matter what you do,
no matter how hard you search for what was there a
    moment ago,
it's nothing but smoke in the wind.

The loss of you…
is unreal.

pathetic, empathetic heart

It has come to my attention that I
love too much
give too much
care too much
drain myself too often
just for a hit of dopamine.
And no matter how hard I try to
change
set boundaries
not care,
my pathetic, empathetic heart still
takes interest
worries
loves.
Many say empathy is a
gift
kindness
sign of humanity.
But for those of us who feel it all,
those of us who take on others'
suffering
struggles
pain

despair,
empathy feels like the ultimate curse.

today, more tears

Today, I cried
at the memory of you
at the loss of what was
at the idea of what should have been.
And I fear,
today
will not be the last day
I soak my sleeves with tears
for you.

eidetic memory

Most of my life,
I've loved the gift of a
photographic memory.
Those small mental images of
loved ones
reminiscent moments
places I've been
joy.
But for more than a year,
having the visual reminder of what is
no more
is the ultimate
affliction.
Pictures and
memories and
emotions
in rare glimpses of a life
that once was.
Only I
see them
remember them
relive them
bemoan them.

But every now and then,
a vision from before
makes me smile.
And it's those eidetic memories,
I hold on to most.

all I wanted was you

Retrospect is a bitch,
but valuable, nonetheless.
In the past thirteen months,
I've had too much time to
reflect
reminisce
regard
all things related to me and you.
My biggest realization after
hours and days and weeks and months
is one key point.
All I wanted was you.
And the deeper I drown in
the infinity pool of recollection,
the more I see how
unhealthy
my need
and love
and dependency
on you was.
I loved you
wholly
fully
immeasurably.

I always wanted a love that was
all-consuming,
but I also wanted a love that was
reciprocated
synergetic
everlasting.
All I wanted was you,
and for a time,
you wanted that too.

haunted

Sometimes, when I lay in bed at night,
eyes closed,
room dark,
not a sound to be heard,
my mind wanders to you.
As if you're there,
next to me,
sleeping quietly
on your side, leg propped on the body pillow and eyes
    masked.
Sometimes, it feels so
real
absolute
definitive,
like I can roll onto my side
and hold you.
But…
that reality no longer exists.
Now…
I am haunted by those lost moments
that slowly slipped away
as we drifted apart.

final blow

When the final blow hit,
I spent minutes in a parking lot,
tears on my face
eyes puffy, burning
again.
And when I tried to distract myself,
when I opened my laptop
in a public place,
those pesky, unwavering, relentless tears
came again
and again
and again.
So I left.
I surrendered to
the pain
the ache
the fact that I will never be the same.
The final blow wasn't even the hardest hit,
but it was the last,
and that fact hurt the most.

leaky faucet

I walked around the store today
and cried.
It came out of
nowhere
and hit like a tidal wave.
While I passed the cookies,
I cried.
While I stared at the drinks,
I cried.
While I looked at things I bought you hundreds of
    times,
I cried.
And if I'm honest,
I'll never not cry
over the reminders of you.

phantom pain

I thought of you
and smiled,
then grew a little
teary-eyed.
I'm not scared to admit that
I miss you
like a limb
like an organ
like an immeasurable piece of my soul.
And when those painful moments
sneak in,
I curse my
mind
body
the very life force in my veins
for betraying me
for twisting and warping my thoughts
for shifting reality and making me less than whole.
I want to think of you
and smile,
but the truth is
whenever I think of you,
I'll always experience phantom pain.

puzzle pieces

coffee / peanut butter cookies / sprinkle cookies / pizza / mac and cheese / massage / sticks / sharks / dinosaurs / blue / 13 / gently / REI / face masks / documentaries, especially those narrated by David Attenborough / Jimmy's / aye, aye, aye / when I make silly voices / phallic-shaped produce / dogs / hash browns / the BDB series / the bank / tattoos / logic / coding / body pillows / my writing/editing focus mode / automations / compote, as said on The Great British Baking Show / pesto / roses / Dark / pierogies / cinnamon rolls / pullover hoodies / Above & Beyond / EDM / fuzzy socks / Reese's / KitKat / fall / spooky season / apple bars / Costco / 1 + 1 / Nicole^2 / Gilmore Girls / Johnny's / ginger beer / Crocs, especially with socks / tubs across from toilets / cheddar / Abe's muffins / nipples! / love you too… three / munchkin / fantasy books / Subaru / beanies / gloves / Oakley / cilantro / crystals / metaphysics / nuts in my mouth / "secret" / silly faces / buttercup / mmm / snow / Voodoo Doughnuts / Valkyrie and Valhalla / Hungry Hungry Hippos / riding mowers / sudoku / puzzles / fabric hair ties / lip balm, especially strong scents that make cats wince / twin flames / soul mates / encouragement… boom! / couscous / Good Intentions / Golden Dinosaur, which is now closed / inside jokes and wordless conversations / pancakes / pizza bites / fluoride-free toothpaste / pretzel buns / hanging with friends / piercing jewelry / burrito blankets / hooded towels / blemish tools / Q-tips / just the tip / Cricut / Zevia / bebe / huni / whales, especially Dory speaking whale / mini donuts / donut holes / Vegas / strawberry banana / no chicken noodle / mini corn dogs / squatty potty / the PNW, especially Vancouver and Portland / motorcycles / rice socks / flower of life / Zen Den / Clearwater / Powell's Bookstore / padre / slippers / te amo / mi esposa / Cards Against Humanity / Pop Tarts / Beauty and the Beast / offering a handkerchief or tissue / Grey Poupon / and so many more...

birthday girl

You reached out
on my birthday,
and if I'm honest,
I was surprised.
But I was also
happy
elated
grateful
to hear from you.
For a time,
we chatted like old friends,
and it felt
nice
normal
hopeful.
It was one of my favorite gifts.

quiet, unconventional celebration

Since the very beginning,
you celebrated my wins with
gusto
applause
your full chest.
Anyone who would listen,
you shared your pride in my accomplishments.
Then,
slowly over time,
little by little,
the pride you once flaunted with ease
waned.
What once was a day of celebration
became a semi-important day,
and I mostly celebrated
alone.
Now,
those big wins,
those major accomplishments,
feel exciting... and not.
Now,
every one of those celebrations is
quiet

unconventional
less magical
not as poignant.
I fear I'll never experience that again.

you—shaped

Oftentimes, I find myself
still
questioning everything.
Although I am healing
physically
mentally,
an emptiness
in the shape of you
exists
persists
gnaws at my soul.
And oftentimes,
I allow myself a moment to
bask
dwell
loiter
reminisce
in the shape of you that will always be
etched on me.

in the periphery

I leave the bathroom
and there you are,
pressed to my side,
in a square frame on the wall.
A conversation sparks about
dogs or
tech or
Gibbs or
insert one of countless things that remind me of you,
and there you are,
happy memories of you spilling from my lips.
After all this time,
you are still
in the periphery
a positive light
on my mind.
And for years to come,
you will remain
in my periphery.

not—so—random texts...
from the past

I probably shouldn't say this, but given different circumstances, I'd keep you forever

#1 personality

#2 eyes

#3 smile

#4 take bullshit from no one

#5 feisty

#6 your drive

#7 intellect

#8 integrity

#9 independence

#1 personality

#2 your honesty

#3 your loyalty

#4 commonalities

#5 your passion and desire

#6 your energy

#7 your compassion

#8 your strength

#9 your beauty

#10 the way I crave you

#11 the way you melt

Never in my life have I connected to a soul as beautiful, as amazing and as inspiring as yours. You soothe my soul and make my heart flutter all at the same time. I couldn't imagine any future days without you in my life, nor would I want to. You are truly my other half, the part that makes me whole. I look forward to the day when I have the beautiful blue double infinity on my left ring finger and you have yours. I really fucking love you, forever and ever, always.

Memory recall… The first night we kissed; first, after school, when you were licking my neck in the parking lot and then, at my old house, we had some deep, passionate kissing going on. Mmmm… Makes me all fluttery inside.

· · ·

Brain fart moment... Are you coming over later or hanging with [redacted]?

Oh darling I'm coming over... I don't know if I can sleep a night without you now

I don't think I could sleep without you either.

I keep smelling your perfume and it's driving me nuts ;)

You're welcome ;)

You just made my entire day better :) chest is all fluttery now

Really fucking love you :) glad I made your entire day better. Muah

You made me melt with just your messages btw

Good :) you make my heart all fluttery. Muah

I love our comfortability, our openness, commonalities, your soothing/calming effect on me, and most of all, having someone who is as much about me as I am about them

You also make my heart fluttery :) muah

Definitely could never have my fill of you

For once in my life, I know without a doubt that I'm exactly where I'm supposed to be with exactly who I'm supposed to be with.

Ditto

I like knowing that I don't feel like I have to have any "me" time because I would rather have you around me all the time

All the moments before you that made me question everything and everyone in life were just putting me on my path toward you.

You are my "me time"

And you as well

There is no me without you

Ditto

Whole heartedly, I love you

All of me loves all of you ;)

Body and soul, I love you completely ;)

Forever and ever, always

Forever and infinite, always

poem of the past

October 19, 2015

404 days ago…
That marks the first moment
my eyes laid upon you.
I was automatically drawn to you.
And I undoubtedly knew
friendship was a given.
Similarities visually apparent,
the start of a new journey,
comfort not so evident.
As days passed,
our paths were more prominently etched
our strongholds were more solidly built
our lives were more intricately intertwined
as we tossed and threw the occasional hint back and
     forth.
Evasion spurred curiosity,
bantering became routine,
an invitation created possibility.
A list of traits,
a detailed attraction out in the open,
luring me
slowly

closer
pulling me in, enraptured.
Enticed, charmed, completely captivated and utterly
    enthralled.
Desirous, I relent,
only to discover
exhilaration in wave after wave.
Practically inseparable,
confessions are made of
equal lust and love,
our souls finally whole, complete.
A kiss to the neck,
I buckle your knees.
I love our effect on each other,
always eager to please.
In the near future,
inevitably it will come true,
forever and ever, always,
we'll both say I do.
Two halves of a whole,
we experience it all the same,
my kindred spirit,
my beautiful twin flame.

the curse of the twin flame

Early in our relationship,
we knew we were more than
soulmates.
Our connection was
physical
mental
emotional
spiritual.
In a brief time, you became my
best friend
lover
sounding board
teacher
healer
constant.
And when you told me
you felt the exact same,
we knew what we
had
were,
twin flames.
Two halves of the same soul,
connected once again.
We talked about this,

discussed what it meant,
and also touched on the
downside and dark side of
twin flames.
Because, as
powerful and
heady and
exciting and
thrilling
as it was to be in your orbit,
there were consequences to finding your
other half.
But we were
confident
determined
resolute
that we would not succumb to the
negativity
toxicity
that came with our connection.
And for a time,
we lived the harmonic life of
twin flames,
blissed out beyond measure.
But somewhere along the line,
the euphoria I experienced with you
faded
darkened
morphed into a stranger.
Unwilling to lose you, I
ignored the shifts
brushed things off as "this" or "that"

deliberately evaded reality,
all to
not ruffle feathers
shed light on the truth
keep you.
The curse of the twin flame is
staying
when it's apparent you need to
leave.
Because our love was so
strong
solid
consuming
dysfunctional
malignant
that we chose to ignore
the widening gorge
to make the other happy.
You will always be my
twin flame,
and sadly,
unfortunately,
nothing more.
But maybe
in another life,
we will get
another chance
and you will be more.
Maybe even
mine
again.

infinite, broken loop

01000110 01101111 01110010 01100101 01110110 01100101
01110010 00100000 01100001 01101110 01100100 00100000
01100101 01110110 01100101 01110010 00101100 00100000
01100001 01101100 01110111 01100001 01111001 01110011
00101110 00100000 01000110 01101111 01110010 01100101
01110110 01100101 01110010 00100000 01100001 01101110
01100100 00100000 01100101 01110110 01100101 01110010
00101100 00100000 01100001 01101100 01110111 01100001
01111001 01110011 00101110 00100000 01000110 01101111
01110010 01100101 01110110 01100101 01110010 00100000
01100001 01101110 01100100 00100000 01100101 01110110
01100101 01110010 00101100 00100000 01100001 01101100
01110111 01100001 01111001 01110011 00101110 00100000
01000110 01101111 01110010 01100101 01110110 01100101
01110010 00100000 01100001 01101110 01100100 00100000
01100101 01110110 01100101 01110010 00101100 00100000
01100001 01101100 01110111 01100001 01111001 01110011
00101110 00100000 01000110 01101111 01110010 01100101
01110110 01100101 01110010 00100000 01100001 01101110
01100100 00100000 01100101 01110110 01100101 01110010
00101100 00100000 01100001 01101100 01110111 01100001
01111001 01110011 00101110 00100000 01000110 01101111
01110010 01100101 01110110 01100101 01110010 00100000
01100001 01101110 01100100 00100000 01100101 01110110

01100101 01110010 00101100 00100000 01100001 01101100
01110111 01100001 01111001 01110011 00101110 00100000
01000110 01101111 01110010 01100101 01110110 01100101
01110010 00100000 01100001 01101110 01100100 00100000
01100101 01110110 01100101 01110010 00101100 00100000
01100001 01101100 01110111 01100001 01111001 01110011
00101110 00100000 01000110 01101111 01110010 01100101
01110110 01100101 01110010 00100000 01100001 01101110
01100100 00100000 01100101 01110110 01100101 01110010
00101110 00101110 00101110 00101110 00101110 00101110

a letter for you

Dear [redacted],

Not sure if you'd expect to hear this or not, but I miss you. So much. Although we haven't stood in the same room for more than a year, although we've barely spoken outside of obligatory text messages, I still love you. So fucking much.

If you thought I cried a lot writing the poetry collection for Shadow, it doesn't remotely compare to the number of tears I've shed while writing about us.

It's been a long, heartbreaking, complicated, confusing, and tumultuous journey since we went our separate ways. But over the past year plus, I've learned a lot about my physical and mental health and how it's impacted me more than I realized. So many times—way more than I care to admit—I've wished there was a way we could've gotten through this together. That something in my mind would've clicked differently at the time. Unfortunately, I don't believe either of us would heal or flourish the way we need to had things not happened the way they did.

As happy as I was that we'd crossed the country

to start a new journey, I also felt lost, scared, lonely, uncertain, and extreme anxiety. For a time, you did your best to assure me everything would be fine. That it'd all work out. But in my unsteady mind, I couldn't see an upside. I tried, really tried, but my thoughts were stuck in this negative loop. And the more my mind twisted, the harder it was to believe anything else. I hate that I couldn't believe anything else.

I can't pinpoint when it happened, but sometime during the first year of the pandemic, we shifted into a life so different from where we began. When I look back, I see now that it was gradual. We were both busy with our own projects. Current me wishes I would've pushed for more quality time, but I also know I never would've because I didn't want to disrupt your focus. I didn't want to be a burden, a nag, or someone you intentionally avoided. I didn't want to make you do something you didn't want to do.

From the start, we spent the majority of our nonworking hours together. The only time we spent with friends without each other was usually when one of us was out of town, which wasn't often or healthy for you, me, or us as a whole.

I've never been an outgoing person unless I'm comfortable with my surroundings. I'm rarely the person to initiate time or conversations with people. But when we first met, you were the perfect extrovert to my introvert. Bold and charismatic. Flirty, intelligent, and wise. Open and honest. You complemented me in unimaginable ways. Hell, people jokingly said we were so similar it was weird. They called us the Bobbsey Twins—two people who are inseparable and often appear to resemble each other. We called it twin flames.

Sadly, at some point, our flame dwindled to an ember. And I hate it. It wasn't you, it wasn't me, but I do believe it was a potent blend of the chemicals between us. The brain chemistry we can only tweak with pills and time and finding whatever it is our souls really need to be whole. In this life, unfortunately, we weren't enough for each other.

A promise I made ten years ago today (the collection's release date) still holds true. I will always love you. Forever and ever, always. I'm honored you were mine, even if it wasn't forever like we wanted.

All I want is for you to be happy. I hope you find joy and fulfillment and the peace you deserve, even if it's without me. Somehow, someway, I will find happiness too. It won't be what it was with you, but it will be the closest I can find.

And if you actually read this, I really hope we find our way back to some form of friendship. It probably won't be for a while, but I hope we come back to it, nonetheless.

I love you.
Forever and ever, always.

[redacted]

thank you

Thank you so much for reading Chemicals Between Us, a contemporary poetry collection. Putting these thoughts and feelings into words after an especially difficult time in my life wasn't easy. To this day, I'm still working through it all. But it means a great deal that you chose to read Chemicals Between Us. A deep, heartfelt thank you and so many virtual hugs.

If you would take a moment to leave a review on the retailer site, Goodreads, BookBub, or wherever you review books, it would mean the world. Reviews help other readers find and enjoy the book as well.

Much love,
    Persephone

MORE BY *persephone*

Ink Veins

Persephone Autumn's debut poetry collection, Ink Veins, explores topics of depression, love, and self-discovery with a raw, unfiltered voice.

Broken Metronome

When the music of the heart dies...

Broken Metronome is an angsty poetry collection full of heartache and the possibility of what may have been.

Slipping From Existence

Would it be so bad to slip from existence? Would it be so bad to give in to the darkness?

Slipping From Existence is a dark poetry collection centered around depression and coping while maintaining a brave face.

Poisonous Heart

Drip fed, little by little, I was young when I got my first taste of poison.

Small doses in heart-shaped packages labeled as love.

I don't remember the very first taste. But that's how poison works.

Beneath Wildflowers

You were the sweetest, most precious surprise.

A soul with a tender heart.

I will love and miss you forever.

As you rest beneath the wildflowers.

CONTEMPORARY & SUSPENSE ROMANCE TITLES

Depths Awakened

A small town romance which captivates you from the start. Mags and Geoff are two broken souls who have sworn off love. Vowed to never lose anyone else. But their undeniable attraction brings them together and refuses to let go.

Distorted Devotion

Free-spirited Sarah lives life to the fullest. When a new love interest enters her life, she starts receiving strange gifts and letters. She doesn't want to relinquish her freedom or new love, but fears the consequences.

Transcendental

A musician in search of his muse and a woman grieving the loss of her husband. Two weeks at an exclusive retreat and their connection rivals all others. Until she leaves early without notice. But he refuses to give up until he finds her again.

The Click Duet

High school sweethearts torn apart. When fate gives them a second chance, one doesn't trust they won't be hurt again. Through the Lens (Click Duet #1) and Time Exposure (Click Duet #2) is an angsty, second chance, friends to lovers romance with all the feels.

Shattered Sun

When your heart is split in two, how do choose who to love more? While Ben, her childhood best friend, and Travis, the hottest cop in Stone Bay, fight for Kirsten's affection, someone else has their eye on her. When she questions everyone and everything, Ben and Travis vow to protect her. In the process, she falls for both men. Before it's too late, she needs to decide which man she loves more.

Tethered Hearts

She will always be mine... even when she belongs to someone else. Shanti Mahal is the love of my life, but over the years I've watched her choose someone else repeatedly. It hurts to watch her choose guys that only want her for one thing. If she chose me, I'd give her everything.

CONNECT WITH
persephone

Connect with Persephone
www.persephoneautumn.com

Subscribe to Persephone's newsletter
www.persephoneautumn.com/newsletter

Join Persephone's reader's group
Persephone's Playground

Follow Persephone online

instagram.com/persephoneautumn

facebook.com/persephoneautumnwrites

tiktok.com/@persephoneautumn

bookbub.com/authors/persephone-autumn

goodreads.com/persephoneautumn

amazon.com/author/persephoneautumn

pinterest.com/persephoneautumn

threads.com/@persephoneautumn

acknowledgments

To my family and friends... I love you all beyond words. The past thirteen months has been difficult and challenging, but your support never wavered. I've had countless ups and downs, and you helped me through them all with love, kindness, strength, and compassion. The path is ongoing, but I know I'll make it because of you.

To my therapist... thank you for encouraging me to write poetry about everything I've been feeling. Usually, I sit on these feelings until they all but explode out of me. But you encouraged me to get it out as I felt it and not to wait.

Rose at Fairy Proofmother Proofreading... you're the absolute best. Poetry is not a genre you usually work with, so I was hesitant to ask you to work on CBU. But I'm so glad you did. Your magic touch always makes my work better. Love you!

My corner of the book community... the past thirteen months was hard, and I'm not alone in feeling this. But I'm so honored to call several of you *friend*. Many reached out to check on me or send a thoughtful message, and every one of those check-ins or normal conversations or positive notes meant more than words. I treasure each of you and our friendship. I am endlessly grateful to know you and have you at my side. Sending all the damn hugs until we see each other in person (cause we will!).

To everyone who picks up one of my books, I love you! Whether Chemicals Between Us is your first Persephone Autumn book or your 30+ read, I never take a single one of you for granted. All the fucking hugs, and I love you!

ABOUT *the author*

USA Today Bestselling Author Persephone Autumn is a proud mom with a cuckoo grandpup. An ethnic food enthusiast who has fun discovering ways to vegan-ize her favorite non-vegan foods. Most days, you'll find her with a tea latte or fruity concoction in her hand. If given the opportunity, she would intentionally get lost in nature.

For years, Persephone did some form of writing; mostly journaling or poetry. After pairing her poetry with images and posting them online, she began the journey of writing her first novel.

She mainly writes romance and poetry, but on occasion dips her toes in other works. Look for her non-romance novel publications under P. Autumn.